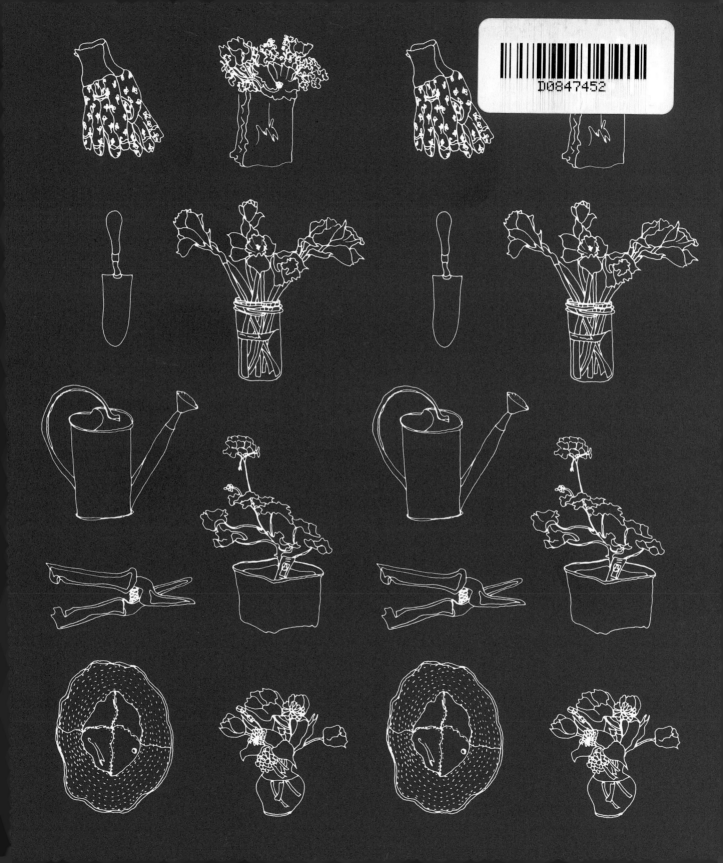

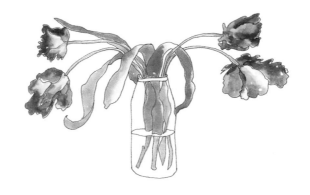

Nan —   March 17, 1995

Happy birthday to you!

love,
john

The Year in Flowers

A DAYBOOK

Watercolors and Text by Katy Gilmore

To Jim and To Crump

Managing Editor: Ellen Harkins Wheat
Editor: Carolyn Smith
Designer: Elizabeth Watson

Flowers illustrated (full-page art): title page, mixed bouquet; opposite Foreword, mixed
bouquet; January, daffodils, amaryllis; February, hyacinth, primroses; March, tulips,
rose tree of China; April, ranunculus, freesias; May, budding branches of chokecherry,
birch, and mountain ash, geranium; June, bachelor's buttons, mixed bouquet;
July, mountain wildflowers, daisies and campanula; August, cosmos, shrub rose;
September, dahlias, rose hip after frost; October, sunflowers, dry chokecherries;
November, stargazer lilies, carnations; December, narcissus, Barbados lily.

Alaska Northwest Books™
An imprint of Graphic Arts Center Publishing Company
Editorial offices: 2208 NW Market Street, Suite 300, Seattle, WA 98107
Catalog and order dept.: P.O. Box 10306, Portland, OR 97210; Tel. 800-452-3032

Printed on acid-free paper in Korea

*This daybook is one of 500 copies issued as a
special edition in support of the Anchorage
Museum of History and Art.*

ACKNOWLEDGMENTS

This daybook contains a potpourri of pictures and words gathered from many years of flower life, part of the life shared with my husband Jim and our sons Chester and William. Thank you three for being a wonderful family and for flower support— from that first garden journal gift and myriad mountain trips to providing the muscle for lawn mowing!

My garden began long ago with the counsel of Alda Grames, and Edee Flynn left in it a legacy of perennials. A "one flower a week for a year" pact with Julie Baugnét led me to draw my first flower chronicles. Frances and William Milner, Sarah White, and Sue Anderson give flowers, flower-bedecked objects, and jars with personality that aid and abet my flower passions. Cheryl and Bob Milner cheer me on. Carol Trout and Cate Freeman provide winter flowers and all-season smiles. I warmly thank all of you.

I am greatly appreciative of Stonington Gallery for years of strong support, redoubled with this project. In making the leap to book, there are those whose words of encouragement made all the difference when *The Year in Flowers* was just a notion, most especially Georgia Blue and Jane Purinton, but also Bobbi Angell, David Carroll, Frances Tenenbaum, and Ann Zwinger. Thanks to each.

It has been a pleasure to work with the stellar people at Alaska Northwest Books. I appreciate Sara Juday's early interest and the vision and skill of each editor: Marlene Blessing, Carolyn Smith, and Ellen Wheat. Betty Watson's sparkling design delights me.

For reading early versions of this text and providing insightful comments, my heartfelt thanks to: Donna Matthews, Debbie Hinchey, Casey Carruth-Hinchey, Patrice Parker, Sandy Underwood, and Sarah McClellen.

I feel a bond with all the owners of my work and speak special gratitude to the following who graciously lent pieces from their collections for reproduction in this book: Jo Ann Asher, Georgia Blue, Marnie and Tom Brennan, Margie Brown, Alex and Carol Bryner, Ruth and Christopher Burkett, Lois Chancellor, Mihoko Hamaguchi, Mary and Mike Manuel, Bridjette March, Cammy Oechsli and Scott Taylor, and Liz and Ken Sherwood.

I thank Carol Bryner in most every category above, and for sharing families, art, and flowers all these years.

FOREWORD

Long before I met Katy Gilmore, several "Gilmores" — Katy's paintings of flowers — graced the walls of our house. They are superb studies, ink and watercolor drawings full of fresh immediacy and vibrant color. Gardener that I fancy myself to be, more than once I've wished I could paint flowers like Katy Gilmore does. But with the rich collection of her art in this book, I think I'll just settle for appreciating her skills.

When you first pick up this daybook, there is no way you can tell that its creator lives in Anchorage, Alaska. Readers may not associate Alaska with a year full of flowers, but well-known Alaskan artist Katy Gilmore reminds us that floral favorites can be enjoyed anywhere through the seasons, and that it is particularly important in a sometimes severe climate to have the aesthetic comfort of beautiful fresh flowers.

In these pages, Katy offers us her vision of a world of flowers we have all come to recognize and know. The hyacinth she renders with such expressive delicacy and intense coloration is just like the one on a windowsill in New York or Anchorage. The poppies, cosmos, and roses could be from a garden in Seattle or a florist in Los Angeles.

When you go beyond the drawings and read the personal reflections Katy has recorded, you quickly find that her responses to flowers are of the sort that readers can share regardless of geographical location. In the inviting pages of this journal, Katy welcomes us to share that sense of joy nature's flowers can give us all.

— Jeff Lowenfels
President, Garden Writer's Association of America
Gardening Columnist, Anchorage Daily News

January

In winter's book, January is a black-and-white illustration. Nature's stark structure is revealed, unsoftened by leaf or color. Birch branches appear as tangles of black lines against the gray daylight or, fattened with hoarfrost, glow white against the night. Spruce trees stand dark on a white winter lawn, each bough's shape defined by its burden of snow. Huge ravens, clad in iridescent black, roost in cottonwood trees frosted white.

In Alaska, first light dawns midmorning on a January day, producing a pale glow over the mountains. This is a serious month—seemingly the most cold, unrelieved by sun, and devoid of easy-to-find flowers. I am restless and housebound. Tired of winter coping, I'm weary of snow-clogged roads, layers of winter clothes, and cold that limits options.

Enchanted by its color, I draw a deep red amaryllis as it blooms. In sequence, on each of two stalks, the calyx splits to reveal four tube-shaped buds. One after another they trumpet wide open, presenting yellow pollen-dusted anthers surrounded by petals of intense color and shape. Planted in November and tardy for the holidays, the blooming amaryllis now provides a welcome daily growing while the world outside remains frozen and still.

Taking the Christmas tree down is a January job, one I let go till the last possible moment, because I'm unwilling to relinquish the colorful lights. Flowers could replace that color, but one of those "rules" (from the interminable list I keep in my head) forbids me to buy grocery store offerings of first daffodils while the tree is still up. Last year I broke my rule on the sixth of January and bought greenhouse-grown daffodils with closed, greenish yellow buds and tightly wrapped stems. They opened on the table next to the dry Christmas tree and a dying poinsettia, their yellow flash coloring January's black-and-white page with dandelion hues and the warmth of sunshine.

❧ JANUARY ❧

2002 : simputy, increase awareness   *January 1*

                                                             January 2

                                                             January 3

                                                             January 4

                                                             January 5

                                                             January 6

                                                             January 7

JANUARY

January 8

January 9

January 10

January 11

January 12

January 13

January 14

❦ JANUARY ❦

January 15

January 16

January 17

January 18

January 19

January 20

January 21

January 22

January 23

January 24

January 25

January 26

....

January 27

....

January 28

....

January 29

....

January 30

....

January 31

My tolerance for weather talk surprises me lately as
my friends and I mine our accretion of weather experience in
conversation. Especially during this cold month, I take notice of
people who like something I don't, the wind or winter in general,
and am surprised by one friend, usually full of equanimity,
who is unsettled by snowstorms. Those who admit a weather
perversity — a sunny personality's fondness for rainy days or an
outdoor lover's relief at the end of summer — intrigue me.

Notes for January

Notes for January

February

During these frozen months, flower shops are treasure houses filled with fragile riches from far-off lands and seasons. To Anchorage by air from California and South and Central America come long-lasting tropical flowers with exotic shapes and an unreal look: protea's leathery leaves and spiky heads, blue-beaked bird-of-paradise with orange plumage, and the variegated pink and green claws of heliconia. Orchids arrive from Hawaii and Thailand. Wondrous tulips from greenhouses in Holland cross the Atlantic and the contiguous United States, and travel up the West Coast to Alaska. Florists know the joyful excess of buckets of delicate larkspur, romantic roses by dozens, boxes of bold gerbera daisies, and multiple stems of stargazers and sunflowers.

I sometimes spend winter Wednesdays with sketchbook and pen at my favorite flower shop. Sitting on a stool surrounded by boundless flower variety, I draw groups of extravagant blooms—dancing ladies of oncidium orchids, tendrils of pale sweet peas, cut amaryllis ready to open. Being so near this bounty gives great pleasure and makes me speculate about our need for flowers. Their beauty and fragility so fittingly attend the significant events of our lives, marking birth and death, and celebrate the small things— giving thanks, bringing cheer. This month, Valentine's Day bouquets stretch from the front door to the back wall, forming a polychrome sea of love greetings.

Winter still imprisons Alaska on Valentine's Day with sub-zero temperatures and frigid north winds. I flee the winter to attend Seattle's annual flower show, and luxuriate in acres of heady, hothouse, indoor blooms. After only a few days in the temperate Puget Sound climate, where crocus and primroses already bloom outside, Alaska's spring beginnings seem more than 1,500 miles away. I return home, cradling a box of primroses in vibrant crayon colors, discouraged to still find so much snow.

But the quality and quantity of light improve this month. The sun now rises high enough above the horizon to give me ever-lengthening hours of work in natural light. If I time the planting right, in addition to imported primroses and florists' freesia to draw, my indoor bulb garden will bloom, releasing the spicy fragrances of narcissus and hyacinth.

❧ FEBRUARY ❧

February 1

February 2

February 3

February 4

February 5

February 6

February 7

❦ FEBRUARY ❦

February 8

February 9

February 10

February 11

February 12

February 13

February 14

❧ FEBRUARY ❧

February 15

February 16

February 17

February 18

February 19

February 20

February 21

February 22

February 23

February 24

February 25

❧

I tend to put flowers in predictable places: on the table
where we eat, in the corner of the kitchen counter, alongside
my work tables. Sometimes, if inspired to honor a visitor or if a gift
bouquet increases my flower worth, I'll place flowers throughout the
house. Respectful of the power of flowers to please me in a glance,
I wish I'd more often set them in unexpected places—on a
teenage son's desk, in the entryway, on every bookshelf—
foiling February with flower treasure!

February 26

February 27

February 28

February 29

Notes for February

Notes for February

March

In spite of the vernal equinox this month, March in Alaska challenges spring's arrival. Longer days with clear skies accompanied by cold nights alternate with snow. Early on a March morning the dim light of 6 A.M. dawn reveals a new snowfall that becomes a blanketing, dizzying blizzard by noon. The arctic wind that blows off glaciers, lifts my hat, and chills my bones is no poet's springtime breeze. This month Alaska remains in winter's grip, so I seek spring in any way I can.

On the first Mother's Day I was a mother, twenty-one years ago, I purchased a rose tree of China to celebrate the day. It has bloomed every year since then, bedecked with soft pink powder puffs of blossoms. Much as I love it flowering outside, I appreciate the rose tree best in March when I can bring budding branches inside to force the blooms. Those branches, along with some from the crabapple tree, look hopeless at first, but soon soften in water and respond to some force within, tricked by the warmth and sunshine on my work table. After a week in the house, the leaves are barely a quarter of an inch long, but tiny jewels of pink flower buds, looking most like embroidered French knots, dot the branches.

Looking for other spring hope on a clear, windy, sub-zero March day, I pluck tulips from buckets at the grocery store, drip them to plastic bag and cart, and whisk them home in my car, which is heated against outdoor reality. But, having endured so many hardships already, the tulips die too quickly. I let them be until the petals fall and stick to tabletops because I admire the pistils and stamens left behind. Their shapes cast shadows in a pool of strong sunshine.

Although the mountains near Anchorage remain winter white against a technicolor blue sky, toward the end of the month the ever-increasing hours of sun trigger breakup beginnings. Breakup, like freezeup, is a historical term with less sway in the modern world. We're no longer dependent on rivers, frozen or thawed, as transportation routes. Nevertheless, new warmth, melting icicles, drips, slush, and thawing remain fervently awaited breakup signs for Alaskans. The beginnings of winter's slow departure bring joy.

One day, I am startled to see crocus shoots sprouting near the house, their green-and-white veined leaves pushing up behind the snow. They won't bloom for weeks, but my heart soars for the coming spring!

❦ MARCH ❦

March 1

March 2

March 3

March 4

March 5

March 6

March 7

❧ MARCH ❧

March 8

March 9

March 10

March 11

March 12

March 13

March 14

❦ MARCH ❦

March 15

March 16

March 17

March 18

March 19

March 20

March 21

March 22

March 23

March 24

❧

Once, on the side of a Dutch bulb box, I read an oddly
translated invitation to enjoy the bulb's "progress of change."
People desire not just the blossom or the bloom, not only color
and show, but the quickening. Daily tending, daily observing of
nature's growth, is renewing. And I recognize it's a blessing of
security and a measure of predictability in life to have
time and a place to enjoy that progress of change.

❦ MARCH ❦

March 25

March 26

March 27

March 28

March 29

March 30

March 31

Notes for March

Notes for March

April

Once past the initial excitement of dramatic melting and the novelty of returned sun, Alaska April seems barren, harsh, and brown. My journal notes the year that children, at an Easter egg hunt in an Anchorage park, got frostbite and were charged by a moose! But recordkeeping also makes me hopeful by reminding me that the period after breakup, before spring greening, can hold moments hinting at the warm seasons to come.

A few blocks from my house, warmth from an old apartment building that faces south and leaks heat from an exposed foundation encourages early daffodils and iris. Behind a melting snowbank against the old part of our house, tulip leaves emerge, looking brave and improbable. An April morning can mean a bitter 12°F chill or a welcome sprinkle that brings a momentary wet-dust, summer smell. Sometimes in the afternoon, I can sit on my front steps and feel hot on my front and cold on my back—like sitting by a campfire on a cold night. Meltwater drips off the eaves. The nearby mountains lose snow from their south-facing slopes, leaving them threadbare and mottled, neither summer purple nor winter white.

When the sun is out in April, it illuminates better than any other time of year, rising high in the sky and shedding a strong, clear light uninterrupted by leaves. I relish these longer days with more hours of light than dark. Since the air is still cold and the ground wet, this is guilt-free sun that doesn't have to be turned into a raked yard, weeded flower bed, or weekend camping trip, but thrills by its very presence.

Alaska spring days lead to laments about dirt and gray. After a winter of heavy snowfall, melted snow's leftover grit covers the city. The sides of the roads are lined with a paste of caked sand. Though still white, the snow in the yard looks hard and artificial. It has melted away from the sidewalk and patches of dead grass are revealed. The cats are happy to have the sidewalk back; they roll and rub regardless of the grit.

This month, in spite of the chill, songbirds will return, geraniums will bloom in local greenhouses, I'll be moved to wash all our windows, and a flood of flowers will arrive from other places with earlier springs. By the end of the month, sweet pea seeds, with their fondness for cold, can be planted next to the house.

APRIL

❦ APRIL ❦

April 1

April 2

April 3

April 4

April 5

April 6

April 7

❧ APRIL ❧

April 8

April 9

April 10

April 11

April 12

April 13

April 14

❧ APRIL ❧

April 15

April 16

April 17

April 18

April 19

April 20

April 21

April 22

April 23

At a lunch to greet a newcomer
to the state and bid farewell to a
longtimer, we speak of Alaska weather
and Alaska living. There is little agreement
among us. Optimistic rebuttals counter
each story of an early winter or late spring.
We share favorite Alaska arrival memories,
along with dreams of departure for warmer
climes. But when the newcomer laments
that the snow she wished away didn't
reveal the green grass she had expected,
there is unanimity in the condolences
offered for the season after
breakup in Alaska.

❦ APRIL ❦

April 24

April 25

April 26

April 27

April 28

April 29

April 30

Notes for April

Notes for April

May

*I*nside, geraniums and dahlia tubers released from their cool, dark places of winter storage sprout shoots and buds in May. Outside, birch trees dabbed with leaves like pointillist dots glimmer in the sunshine. Hard rains bring greening grass and blooming bulbs. I can pick my own tulips, fragrant narcissus, and daffodils, and marvel at their strength and variety.

Pale yellow tulips open first against the house. In the midmorning sunshine they yawn wide, revealing currant-red throats with smudges of black. The tulip and daffodil display continues all month and into June. Some days I count my bounty, compare sizes (big meaty tulips and tiny budlike ones) and list colors (canary yellow, tomato red, rich burgundy, and a panoply of pinks). My favorite pink, a warm and delicate hue with opaque paleness, evades capture with transparent watercolor.

Birds, courting and nest building, wake us early and attend the welcome outdoor cleaning-up and preparing work. I focus more and more on the outside, raking old leaves and birch twigs, clearing away winter clutter of snow shovels and car heater cords. I have pent-up energy after a winter without yard work and feel the joy and hope of new beginnings.

Flower bed soil smells alien and desirably organic after months of frozen ground, and eyes starved by winter's monochrome feast on tiny beginnings of perennials. I greet the perennials like old friends, proud we've survived the winter, happy to see them so early. The green leaves of Jacob's ladder, columbine, three kinds of daisies, bachelor's buttons, and my particular specialty, never-blooming iris, decorate the newly cleaned-up beds. Blossoms of butter yellow trollius, shocking blue scilla, and a purple primrose flash complementary colors.

May builds to Memorial Day weekend, often the true start of outdoor planting, and suddenly the world spins faster with light and growing. Having started no annuals indoors (an Alaska necessity), I make forays to local greenhouses, which glow with slightly filtered but uniquely luminous light, redolent of thousands of plant beginnings. I fill a cardboard box with pink geraniums for the front porch pots; crinkly four-packs of beloved petunias, pansies, and cosmos for containers; and stock and nicotiana for a fragrant border. I also choose a scabiosa and a red lily to try in favored spots on the south side of the house and a new pair of pruners as a springtime treat.

❦ MAY ❦

....

May 1

....

May 2

....

May 3

....

May 4

....

May 5

....

May 6

....

May 7

May 8

May 9

May 10

May 11

Perennials speak all the best words of
spring—reawakening and returning—the first outdoor
growing in a northland May. I look for them anxiously
as proof my world tilts again to the sun. New leaves from old
roots call out their names and characters with hints of blossom colors
to come: bachelor's buttons green with gray, trollius green by
yellow. On sunny May days the plants grow inches by
nightfall, racing to bloom, while annuals still
seek shelter indoors.

❧ MAY ❧

May 12

May 13

May 14

May 15

May 16

May 17

May 18

❦ MAY ❦

May 19

May 20

May 21

May 22

May 23

May 24

May 25

❦ MAY ❦

May 26

May 27

May 28

May 29

May 30

May 31

Notes for May

Notes for May

June

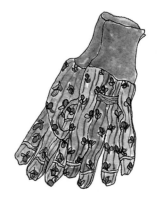

$\mathscr{G}$arden" is a relative term. My garden combines within a city lot a miscellany of narrow flower beds hugging the house, plants in containers, and volunteer seedings. I suppose too many of the plants remain individuals, and the garden lacks the vision of a design plan. Over the years, my priority was too often the painting of the product, rather than the process of gardening.

I always place plantings close together, hopeful of instant color. But this year I've resisted flower-tag descriptions or four-pack blooms and instead accept impatiens near a shaded bench and give up zinnia dreams. On the stumps of the old chokecherry tree, where they have a chance at sun, I put pots of pink pansies with old-fashioned ruffled faces next to pansies whose true-blue petals surround a central yellow dot. I rig wider perches on the stump and add potted petunias in royal purple and bright red, also pale pink and white. Visible from the house, they inspire painting thoughts. Twelve frilly upright cosmos are positioned in a half barrel. I picture dancing flowers in August.

Waiting for me to form a plan, my plants mature and begin to shape them-selves into a satisfying garden vision. I appreciate every earthworm, each lily spear that survives and pokes above ground, all the bouquets of crabapple blossoms and lilac offered up to the house, and the self-seeded pinks that stand tall each year by the sidewalk and between patio stones. The peonies, after years of settling in, finally have buds. One of last year's experimental lilies multiplied fourfold. The colors of divided and transplanted perennials light up my garden: hot pink bleeding hearts, orange hawkweed, columbine in mauve and pink and creamy white, saucer-sized orange poppies with midnight blue centers.

I can draw outside now, with mosquitoes keeping me company. Flies pollinate the chocolate lily; industrious wasps build a nest dangling from a birch branch outside my studio window. Robins are back. (The appeal of our lawn's worms must win out over cat danger.) When a fat and unwary baby robin falls from the nest and spends time on the ground being fed by his parents, we confine the disgruntled cats to the house.

By mid-month's solstice I am rich with flowers to paint and yard jobs to do. We garden late in the evening here. It's a joy to weed the Jacob's ladder on the west side of my house at 11 P.M. with the sun still high. We have two Junes' worth of daylight in this month of longest days — 19 hours and 21 minutes on summer solstice!

❦ JUNE ❦

....

June 1

....

June 2

....

June 3

....

June 4

....

June 5

....

June 6

....

June 7

❧ JUNE ❧

June 8

June 9

June 10

June 11

❧

Like a lot of people, I prefer the flowers of English
cottage gardens described in nineteenth-century novels. Informal
and profuse, tall, fragrant flowers—hollyhock, cottage pinks,
foxglove, Canterbury bells, and stock—combine their colors and
shapes to please in perfect health and continual bloom. Once,
on a family trip to an English village, during an after-dinner stroll,
we heard strains of Mozart floating over a stone wall, the
clink of china, and low voices. I'm sure beyond that stone
wall grew one of those lush and literary gardens.

❧ JUNE ❧

June 12

June 13

June 14

June 15

June 16

June 17

June 18

❧ JUNE ❧

June 19

June 20

June 21

June 22

June 23

June 24

June 25

June 26

June 27

June 28

June 29

June 30

Notes for June

Notes for June

July

The Chugach Mountains, Anchorage's eastern horizon, are a touchstone and dramatic presence in all seasons. Remote and unforgiving in winter white, they beckon in summer with slopes and valleys clad in velvet of purple and green. Snow patches linger until June and fresh snow falls by August's end. But July contains mountain days with cloudless blue sky and tundra turned flowery.

One summer I spent every Monday in the mountains, watching the season's succession of flowers. Summer's flower show begins with tiny pink blossoms of bog blueberry appearing the first week of June and ends with late-blooming blue gentian in September. In lower elevations showy introductions, such as neon-orange Icelandic poppies and loud yellow dandelions, edge parking lots and trailheads alongside stately indigenous plants—wild rhubarb with white blossom clusters and umbelliferous cow parsnip. Bordering streams and wet habitat, wild geranium, monkshood, and lupine in shades of purple form lush drifts. Higher, on steep scree slopes, the hardy plant mountaineers subsist in the harshness of gravel—mountain harebell, oversized blue cups on wire-thin stems, and yellow-cowled capitate lousewort.

My favorite patch is an amphitheater of flowers, a protected alpine garden encircled by mountain hemlock and surfaced with hummocks of thick spongy tundra. The first time I found the spot, I thrilled to identify the flowers: the blues of chiming bells, common harebell, and tall Jacob's ladder mix with nearby yellow dots of potentilla blossoms. A cylinder of fuzz and serrated leaves identify woolly lousewort early in the year; pink flowers will follow. Blossom heads of valerian—Victorian posy bouquets of exquisite magenta buds—open to tiny flowers. Nodding stems of pale pink twinflowers tip their twosomes in greeting beside groups of upright star gentian. Sitka burnet is all stamens without petals arranged as a softly bristling spike. Like Siberian aster, coastal fleabane enjoys a familiar daisy shape and lavender-pink petals.

Mountain flowers look too delicate to exist above treeline and survive baking sun, high winds, and punishing winter, but their coping tricks are many. Their small size and compact growth habits conserve energy, and because most are perennials, their established roots assure an early start in the spring. Alpine plants efficiently flower and disperse seed within the brief mountain growing season. Those plants producing berries ripen in August when bearberry leaves carpet the fall tundra with scarlet.

❦ JULY ❦

.... *July 1*

.... *July 2*

.... *July 3*

.... *July 4*

.... *July 5*

.... *July 6*

.... *July 7*

❧ JULY ❧

July 8

July 9

July 10

July 11

July 12

July 13

July 14

❦ JULY ❦

July 15

July 16

July 17

July 18

July 19

July 20

July 21

❦ JULY ❦

July 22

July 23

July 24

July 25

July 26

July 27

July 28

.... *July 29*

.... *July 30*

.... *July 31*

❦

A letter arrived today from my
English illustrator friend who writes
from a painting trip to Italy. A garden
there has "nightingales, cuckoos, jasmine,
green lizards, and two grass snakes."
When writing back, I'll describe
the hummocks of flowers we
found on a hike to Crow Pass while
scrambling above the pass. Scattered
in the scree, only a foot in diameter,
each patch was a miniature alpine garden
in itself, supporting heather,
pink campion blossoms, and, best of
all, attending butterflies.

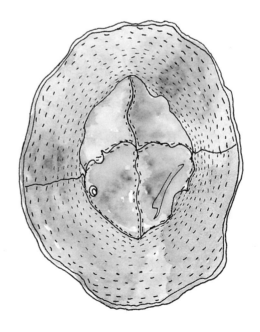

Notes for July

Notes for July

*A*ugust

By late August, hard rains in the city can mean snow in the mountains. Clouds lift one day and reveal mountains draped in a snow cloak, shaped by peaks and valleys, hemmed at the bottom in a straight white line. This snow signal, called "termination dust" by Alaskans, hurries the completion of seasonal jobs and warns of winter's approach. But early in August, before the warning, gardens are in full flower.

I am thankful this month for all the efforts of Anchorage gardeners. On trips about town I enjoy the products of their passion—gardeners' gifts to passersby. In neighborhoods transformed by flowers and softened by summer, I spot my favorites: sunflowers decorating a church, a rectangular bed with lilies on a lawn's east side, raised beds with tangles of perennials, window boxes full of petunias, bedded-out begonias, and cosmos any place! Everywhere sweet peas climb fences and trellises on south and west sides of houses, happily thriving in the sun. Around the corner from my house, I stop to admire a yellow and blue wonderland, a yard teeming with sunflowers, calendula, and bachelor's buttons.

Anchorage turns tourist town in summer. Even in the beginnings of the rainy season, August visitors delight in the city's plantings. All about town, flowers burst forth to beautify the cityscape. An alphabet of annuals from alyssum to zinnia stretches between the museum and a busy three-lane street. The town square, the grounds of the main library, and hundreds of hanging baskets are laden with thousands of flowers to celebrate summer. At Kincaid Park's rock garden, low plants stairstep up boulders to tall pink cosmos, providing unexpected, cultivated beauty beside wooded trails populated by bikers, runners, and moose.

These orderly planted annuals wax against the ubiquitous background of Alaska fireweed, whose exuberant magenta blossoms wane past cotton candy–textured seedpods by month's end. Mid-August, flocks of geese begin to gather, taking whirling practice flights from city staging areas, warming up in preparation for their migrations. One morning, a few yellow leaves dot the lawn. Daylight hours have been steadily lost since June 21; real darkness falls at night for the first time in months. After so much daylight, it is startling to need a flashlight in the tent or headlights on the car.

❦ AUGUST ❦

August 1

August 2

August 3

August 4

August 5

August 6

August 7

❧ AUGUST ❧

August 8

August 9

August 10

August 11

August 12

August 13

August 14

August 15

August 16

August 17

❦

In my earliest flower memory
I was in the third grade. I played the wild rose
in a school play about a garden and the
Prince of Flowers. A big, pink, cardboard-and-
crepe-paper petal arrangement covered me from
chin to knees. The wild rose is not welcome in the
garden amongst the real flowers, of course,
but I can't remember the play's denouement.
Since I was the only American "weed" in a
class of Canadian blossoms, I just
remember that it all felt right.

❧ AUGUST ❧

August 18

August 19

August 20

August 21

August 22

August 23

August 24

❧ AUGUST ❧

August 25

August 26

August 27

August 28

August 29

August 30

August 31

Notes for August

Notes for August

September

On a clear day promising a cold night in early September, I gather all I can from the flower beds in anticipation of a frost. Cosmos and dahlias in vases of their own adorn my table. Smaller jars hold end-of-the-year mixes: the last of the pinks, hawkweed, calendula, and pansies. Another jar contains sweet peas. I pass by the petunias; they suffer from hard rains, which have melted their petals into slimy goneness.

Each favorable day in an Alaska September is a gift. We can have frost as early as September 10. Labor Day backpacking in the mountains might end in a snow-covered tent. These are days in which to savor the last moments of summer, drink final cups of tea on the porch in the afternoon, and appreciate early morning bike rides, soon to end, as daylight comes later each morning. By September 21, the autumn equinox, we have begun our brief fall. On average, the first snow falls in Anchorage on October 7. Each day could be a garden's last.

Still searching for summer, I visit the Alaska Botanical Garden. Only recently opened, the gardens greet me as sun-dappled glades embraced by a guardian conifer and birch forest. Established gardens like this one have begun to change the face of the city. This botanical garden, formal by frontier standards, implies a settled land. Some might find such civilizing threatening and limiting. I am grateful to those who plant.

The only other visitor this day is a moose, who dismisses me with a glance and moves into the trees. I walk the paths between gardens, testing the sunny bench by each. Most plants are past bloom, and a recent hard frost has withered many others. Clumps of dianthus, crowns of painted daisies, spikes of iris leaves, patterned leaves of foxglove, and tangled mats of creeping baby's breath dot the rich soil of raised beds. Carefully placed plant labels—Shasta daisies, aconitum, alpine aster, and delphinium—make it easy to imagine summer glories. But today, blue sky and yellow birch color the garden and Alaska's autumn.

In my backyard on these windy fall days, the tree canopies are shrinking. It isn't so much that the leaves fall, though they do, but they are shriveling. The spaces between leaves grow larger, revealing the framework of branches. I see sky that was blocked by green all summer.

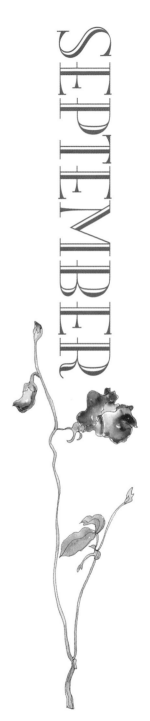

SEPTEMBER

❧ SEPTEMBER ❧

September 1

September 2

September 3

September 4

September 5

September 6

September 7

❦ SEPTEMBER ❦

September 8

September 9

September 10

September 11

September 12

September 13

September 14

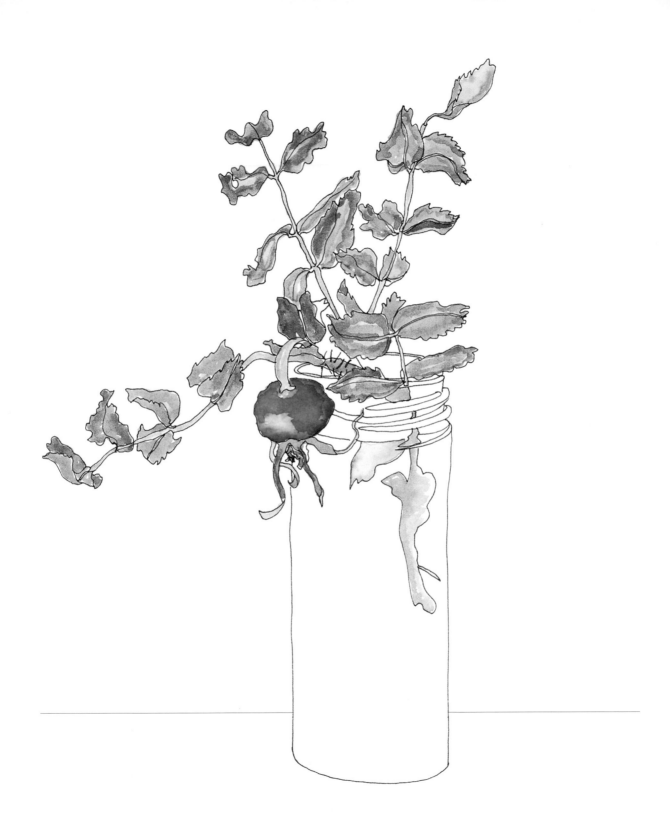

❧ SEPTEMBER ❧

September 15

September 16

September 17

September 18

September 19

September 20

September 21

September 22

September 23

Parts of town are landscaped in
cement—cinder-block buildings, dusty
paved streets, blacktopped parking lots.
By late summer, nature steps in to embellish
the hardness. My favorite spot is found on a
street mid-town, at the base of a crooked sign.
There, lively stems of squirreltail grass grow
among soft blossoms of butter-and-eggs.
When caught at a stoplight, I admire
nature's design. Snapdragon shapes of
cadmium-yellow-pale butter and
cadmium-yellow-dark eggs are patterned
with graceful fronds of squirreltail grass.

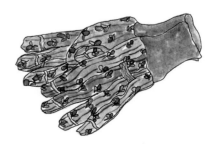

❧ SEPTEMBER ❧

September 24

September 25

September 26

September 27

September 28

September 29

September 30

Notes for September

Notes for September

October

*B*otanists say winter officially arrives when the average temperature falls below 43°F. Thus, winter in Alaska begins in October. Some snow always falls this month, but not enough to enliven the fading daylight. Even southern exposures in my house brighten only briefly while the sun moves low on the horizon. I fantasize about moving, envy geese and whales their southward treks. I tell myself this month contains days perfect for working indoors (rain pours on nearly bare trees and leaf-covered ground), but grieve for sun and light curtailed now for months.

Cleaning up the garden on a windy, clear day, I pick a last sweet pea and scattered pansies, extract frosted annuals, mulch around perennials, and find new places for bulbs. My hands are cold planting bulbs, but with each I connect this fall day to spring. Flowering bulbs, because of their longevity and reliable reappearance after winter dormancy, capture the continuity inherent in gardening. I know a bulb garden where tulips, planted secretly one fall at the news of a baby-to-be, put forth into the world the next spring, right along with the new child. The descendants of those originals, the tough kind of yellow and red tulips that willingly spread, continue years later to delight. This year I've paid attention to my spring journal notes encouraging me to buy many bulbs for planting: more and varied tulips, and crocus and miniature daffodils to bury close to the foundation. I cover the garden with leaves from raking, a first layer of insulation. Snow protects better and will come soon.

From outside I bring in the "gone-bys" to paint: a cluster of mountain ash berries, dangling rich orange-red; chokecherries and a rose hip, captivating shapes when wizened by frost. A trip to the florist yields sunflowers. The geraniums are inside now, where they'll bloom for a while and then give up for lack of light. I board them out to a friend with patience and a warm garage. The narcissus bulbs I've planted in pebbles and water grow quickly. I'm glad I have more in the refrigerator to start later.

Magpies scout chokecherries and crabapples; Steller jays visit the mountain ash. A squirrel harvests its winter supplies, repeating an elevated route along high fence, tree, roof, tree again, and garage (home base). Waxwings pause here in the fall, heading south. Twittering and pulsing flocks visit repeatedly until all the berries and crabapples are gone. They bask in treetops and fly off as a group when one startles. Too quickly they depart for the year.

❧ OCTOBER ❧

October 1

October 2

October 3

October 4

October 5

October 6

October 7

❦ OCTOBER ❦

October 8

October 9

October 10

October 11

October 12

October 13

October 14

....

October 15

....

October 16

....

October 17

❦

At October's freezeup, since I neither migrate nor hibernate,
much autumn preparation in the natural world excludes me.
Staying behind and awake, I prepare anew to negotiate the darkness
and the cold—making winter adjustments to my search for flowers,
light, and warmth. On Halloween night, I recognize kindred spirits
in the gauzy-skirted fairies and legging-clad Robin Hoods
who come to the door. Their make-believe encumbered by
parkas and boots, they adapt to the north.

❦ OCTOBER ❦

October 18

October 19

October 20

October 21

October 22

October 23

October 24

OCTOBER

October 25

October 26

October 27

October 28

October 29

October 30

October 31

Notes for October

Notes for October

November

*T*his month, welcome new snow muffles the announcement of true winter's arrival. The lawn becomes a clean sweep of white, reflecting light. Snowflakes swirling in streetlights and porch lights distract me from the dark. With November's winter days, the search for flowers becomes more necessary to lift my spirits and harder to accomplish in an out-of-season world.

November flowers in Alaska are imported from elsewhere, cosseted on their journey, and limited in supply. Even grocery store flowers, usually the highlight of my frequent shopping trips, look tired to me—cellophane-wrapped bunches of carnations and mystery bouquets, a couple of ready-to-bloom amaryllis braving blasts of cold air in their spot by the door. Searching for winter gardens, I visit a flower wholesaler with florist friends, attend an orchid society meeting, and view a display of garden club flower arrangements. My eye longs for the intricacies of flowers and isn't satisfied by the single limp lily on my desk, though its fragrance has delighted me for days.

Images on paper or china or textile please my eye. In November I search out flower images captured on fabric, wrapping paper, tin boxes, postcards, seed packets, children's drawings, and sheets of postage stamps. Flowers ornament and embellish, bringing their color, shape, and associations to winter life. More than anything, they make something special: flowers embroidered on a baby's overalls, stylized patterns on quilts or rugs, a forget-me-not teacup, flowery chintz or calico print. From under a pile of bills and magazines, a flower envelope catches my eye—a ring of flowers embedded in handmade paper adorns the card inside.

Flower books keep me company on a winter afternoon. When I read gardeners' adventures, descriptions of flowers, or garden plans, I am happily transported to other places and seasons. Pictures magnify that experience— formal portraits of single species, casual bouquets in whimsical containers, photos of extravagant gardens. I stroll through the pages and pretend I might have such gardens, grow such flowers. All seems possible in the impossibility of frozen November ground.

At 3 P.M. twilight with snow falling gently, I defy winter with tea made from flowers—jasmine or chamomile—in a flower-strewn pot.

❦ NOVEMBER ❦

November 1

November 2

November 3

November 4

November 5

November 6

November 7

November 8

November 9

November 10

❧

I am fooled, then insulted, by red plastic tulips on a winter doorstep, or battered fabric fuchsias hanging in pots. Encountering the artificial dashes all my wonder and appreciation for a fragile organism in a hostile environment. Real flowers engage my mind and my heart: who planted them, who cares for them, how much sunshine do they need, how much water, will they last the winter?

❦ NOVEMBER ❦

November 11

November 12

November 13

November 14

November 15

November 16

November 17

❧ NOVEMBER ❧

November 18

November 19

November 20

November 21

November 22

November 23

November 24

❧ NOVEMBER ❧

November 25

November 26

November 27

November 28

November 29

November 30

Notes for November

Notes for November

December

ecember quickens with celebrations, bringing light and color to the darkened North. Arctic conditions outdoors, cold, dark, and harsh, contrast with the inside festive world of warmth, cheer, color, and the richness of holidays with family and friends. We turn inward this month, confined to the house by lack of light as much as cold. The dim daylight, lasting just five hours and 28 minutes on the winter solstice, passes too quickly.

The first time I bought flowers in December, greenhouse tulips from Holland, I drew them where they sat, extravagant and improbable, on the desktop with the holiday wrappings. Flowers in a December setting, as gift or decoration, prove rare and valuable beyond their summer worth. Some flowers, like the unseasonal tulips, seem incongruous and out of place this time of year; other winter plants have long-standing links to merrymaking. Fragrant spruce boughs and a Christmas tree serve as reminders of forest and growing things. The tree's lightbulbs of yellow and blue, red and green, provide a needed jolt of color. So do poinsettias—a big red or a tiny pink one—and a blooming amaryllis. This year the refrigerator holds a freesia sprinkled with sparkle dust nestling on shredded paper—a gift for my son's date to the high school winter dance, aptly named the Snow Ball.

Always, boxes of fresh green holly arrive by airmail from Washington State, the end of each branch carefully wrapped. The branches harbor an organic smell, reminiscent of summer, alien to December. I trim the holly, prick my fingers, happily set it all over the house, and give it away. The red berries entertain the winter-bored cats who pounce and chase them as they shrivel and fall.

To a winter solstice tea party, a friend brings red tulips in a tiny vase wrapped with wires of glittering stars; another bears narcissus bulbs in a green glass pot. Frosty dark outside makes the warmth of candles and firelight a welcome and necessary part of the party by midafternoon. There is real enthusiasm to mark the winter solstice in Alaska dark. From now on daylight will be expressed in gains rather than losses. We honor the year's nadir and welcome the light!

DECEMBER

❦ DECEMBER ❦

December 1

December 2

December 3

December 4

December 5

December 6

December 7

December 8

December 9

December 10

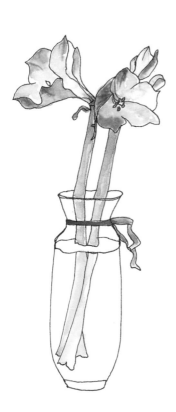

❦

In December my Christmas cactus,
uninspired and ignored most of the year, holds jubilee.
Responding to the cold of the window, it puts
forth intricate shocking pink blossoms that open to white. I
am always surprised by the cactus's stalwart loyalty,
but even more so by the Barbados lily. The lily lived here
for years before it suddenly sent out a stalk crowned
with a delicate, demure orangy-pink blossom.
Customarily, it buds as a holiday gift and blooms
to welcome the new year!

❦ DECEMBER ❦

December 11

December 12

December 13

December 14

December 15

December 16

December 17

❧ DECEMBER ❧

December 18

December 19

December 20

December 21

December 22

December 23

December 24

❦ DECEMBER ❦

December 25

December 26

December 27

December 28

December 29

December 30

December 31

Notes for December

Notes for December

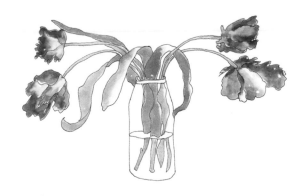

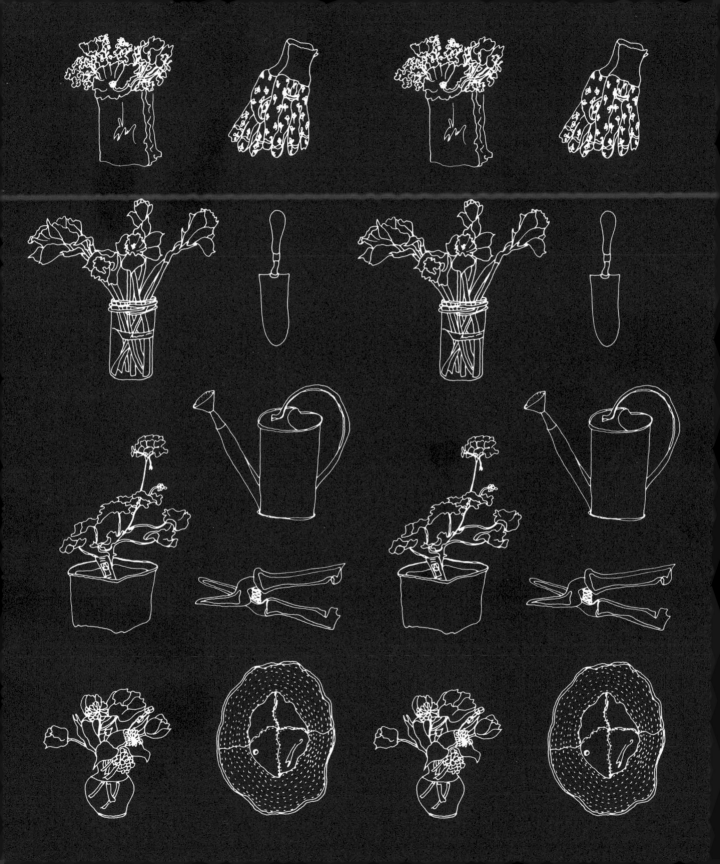